M000303479

Exultation

A POEM CYCLE
IN CELEBRATION OF THE SEASONS

Monza Naff

These poems are also published in the
collection *Healing the Womanheart*
by Monza Naff.

Wyatt-MacKenzie Publishing
15115 Highway 36, Deadwood, Oregon 97430
toll free 1-877-900-9626 *www.WyMacPublishing.com*

Designed by Nancy Cleary, www.designscapestudio.com
Watercolor Illustration by Katherine Witteman
Calligraphy by Carol Erickson Dubosch
Printed and bound at Eugene Print, Eugene, Oregon

Copyright ©Monza Naff 1999. All Rights Reserved.

ISBN: 0-9673025-1-X

for
Mama,
Rose Mary Fishback,
who embodies
saying "YES!" to Life,
all of it

ACKNOWLEDGMENTS

I am profoundly grateful to Nancy Cleary,
Katherine Witteman, and Carol Erickson
DuBosch, who have taught me, through the
creation of this book of words and visual art,
that collaboration among women — across
miles and difference — can transcend a
mere sharing of skills to become an
intimate weaving of sister spirits. — M.N.

Nancy Cleary received her degree in Graphic Design from RHODE ISLAND SCHOOL OF DESIGN in 1990. She has operated her own design company, *DesignScapes Studio,* in Oregon since 1992. In 1999 she started a publishing company to assist artists, poets, writers, musicians and speakers in the design, production and marketing of their creative projects.

Katherine Witteman is inspired by a love of language, an enthusiasm for bold color, and the magical combination of words and pictures. Her art is meant to capture the eye and hold the heart. She works in her studio, *Dancing Heart*, in Portland, Oregon.

Carol Erickson DuBosch loves to make letters and teach others the joy of writing with wet ink. Carol is a professional lettering artist who works, plays and teaches in Portland, Oregon.

TABLE OF CONTENTS

Praying for Release

Autumn,

urge me to drop
every leaf I don't need—
every task or habit I repeat
past its season,
every sorrow I rehearse,
each unfulfilled hope I recall,
every person or possession
to which I cling—
until my branches are bare,
until I hold fast
to nothing.

Blow me about
in your wild iron sky,
crush
all that's puffed up,
fluff
all that in me needs
to go to seed,
send my shadows to sleep.

Tutor me
through straining night winds
in the passion of moan and pant,
the gift of letting go
at the moment
of most abundance—
in the way of
falling apples, figs, maple leaves, pecans.

Open my eyes
to your languid light,
let me stare in your face
until I see no difference
between soar and fall,
until I recognize
eternity
in single breaths,
faint whispers of cool air
through lungs.

Show me the way
of dying
in glorious boldness ~
yellow, gold, orange, rust, red, burgundy, brown

Praying for a Thaw

Winter,

sing me a symphony
in wind,
drum whole notes of rain
on my head.

Shake me
through the fog of sleep,
rock me to the rhythm
of my own true pulse.
Flood me
with your holy water,
make me
gasp for breath.

Speak to me
in a language of diamonds,
single drops of rain
in sunlight.
And I will respond
from my watery depths,
flowering, shining.

Wake me
to worship my garden.
I will follow the pace
of filtered light,
discover a new rainbow,
this one white, beige, brown, gray, black.
I want to dance with skeletons,
wet, bare limbs and hips,
recite, over and over,
moon chants I learn in my sleep
through long night mists and storms.

Whisper to me
the cleansing secret
of torrent and gale,
Drench me
and pull at my roots.

Carry me away
on your fierce sky music,
whirl me in the current
of raging rivers,
foamy waves.

Teach me to dream
hot life blood
into my cold fingers.
Call me
with your cool tongue,
and I will reply with fire.

Praying to Break Through

Spring,

wake me to grow,
stretch and tremble,
break up my clay,
crumble me fine.
Warm all my rows,
the hills and furrow paths,
as you work me, wet or dry.

Send for me, soft,
in the language
of lambs' tongues,
velvet oh's and ah's.
And I will come out
from my winter-slowed cave,
whispering, aching.

Push me through
steaming earth, rich loam,
Stir my roots deep
from beneath.
Quicken my core
with your hot hands, and
I will sing spirals of seeds.

Heave me up
into the sun,
pull me to the surface
by my pale green shoots.
Shout your YES!
into my bulbs,
fill my limbs with light.

Pour me into
the fragrance of change,
make me fertile and strong.
Open my fists
of tightly furled petals
into the glory of
white · green · pink · red.

Feed me full
of the promise of bloom,
take all of me you need.
Train me by tendril
to grow, grow still. I want
to learn your cycle by cell:
want · need · must · will.

Praying to Bear Fruit

Summer,

shine on my breasts,
in my hair, down my back
with the hot blue juice of your sky.
From earliest morning to late-coming night
may you boil, roil
in the blood
'til you burn all away
but perfume.

In soft night come close,
wet the garden
and field with my sweat,
the sap of bent back and knee,
and the dew from
just enough cloud.
I want to wake
to breezes bursting with
tomato, marigold, mint, peony, basil,
geranium and dill.

Fill the forests, the mountains,
the lakes and the plains
with your
honey gold heat
to warm all wanderers,
wheat to see the pilgrims through
from harvest to bloom.

Nourish the babies,
old women and men,
and the swaggering, sweltering youth
with your bounty,
a miracle
of just three moons.
Teach, if you will, delight by mouth,
utter joy of suck and chew and gulp
of the just right ripe.
And may we all bear fruit.

Pierce the earth
with primary colors—
blazing red, yellow, blue and green—
and lazy shades
of dawn and dusk—
moss, cornflower, pink, lavender, melon.
In your silent puncture,
pulsing,
heal us to the heart.

Let us,
oh, get us
to leap,   sing,   laugh,
and lie in the grass,
fall to our knees,
and turn somersaults
in your gleaming,
streaming
light.

TO ORDER

Contact IGS, or call the Publisher *toll free* 877-900-9626
or order online at *www.WyMacPublishing.com*

Also published by *Wyatt-MacKenzie Publishing*:
Monza Naff's **Healing the Womanheart**

ISBN 0-9673025-0-1, 152 pages
PRICE: $14.95 + *$1.50 shipping & handling*

Healing the Womanheart
is available on audiotape
with the poet reading
selections from this
collection

PRICE: $10.95
+ *$1.50 shipping & handling*

4100-10 Redwood Rd., #316
Oakland, CA 94619

510-336-0449 *Fax:* 510-336-0450
e-mail: MonzaNaff@aol.com

INNER GROWTH SERVICES

*Classses, workshops, and retreats in meditation and
writing, spiritual formation and ritual making.*